Freeze Tag

Wesleyan New Poets

Freeze Tag

Marea Gordett

Wesleyan University Press ⬦ Middletown, Connecticut

Copyright © 1984 by Marea Gordett

Grateful acknowledgment is made to the following publications, in
which some of these poems appeared: *Chicago Review*, "1943," *Cin-
cinnati Poetry Review*, "The Air Between Two Deserts," *Denver Quar-
terly*, "Grandmother," "In the Shoe Factory," "Marriage," *Mississippi
Review*, "The Boy Named Several," *MSS*, "Garden," *The Nation*,
"Family Living in Abandoned Cave," *Partisan Review*, "When I Was
Young," *Sun Dog*, "Norwegian Morning." "The Air Between Two Des-
erts" also appeared in *Pushcart Prize V* (1980–81), and "Marriage" in
Anthology of Magazine Verse and Yearbook of American Poetry.

All inquiries and permissions requests should be addressed to the
Publisher, Wesleyan University Press, 110 Mt. Vernon Street, Middle-
town, Connecticut 06457.

Distributed by Harper & Row Publishers, Keystone Industrial Park,
Scranton, Pennsylvania 18512.

Library of Congress Cataloging in Publication Data

Gordett, Marea. Freeze tag.

  (Wesleyan new poets)
  I. Title. II. Series.
PS3557.O645F7 1984   811'.54   84-2250
ISBN 0-8195-2117-5 (alk. paper)
ISBN 0-8195-1118-8 (pbk.: alk. paper)

Manufactured in the United States of America

First Edition

In loving memory of my grandmother,
Esther Kramer, and with deep appreciation
to my teachers, especially James Tate and
Joel Conarroe

Contents

III   Freeze Tag

❧ I

The wind, the wind, the wind blows high.
The snow is falling from the sky.
Maisie Drummond says she'll die
For want of the Golden City. . . .

—CHILDREN'S JINGLE

Desire

All we can remember is desire.
The way the pears sit in a raku
bowl, immune from touch
and perfectly ripe. Dawn
riding on the sea—
and dreaming of its color, how we rise
to swim. Nothing resembles anything
else, we want only
new ways to love
memory. Your smile
sleeping on another face,
dreaming its way back
to childhood, that first hunger.

A painter looking past a curtain
to the hills
knows the feel of running,
a girl pulling a comb through her hair
is drunk with longing, your shoulder
just out of reach slips past
in the shape of a hill
or russet fruit on a table,
impossible to eat.

✣ When I Was Young

I always loved the word *foothills*.
A little shape of nothing stands in the hills
pygmying out its life. On the other
hand, I hate the words *pretty*, *cuneiform*, and *hog*.
Today, driving to the pretty foot-
hills, a cuneiform hog dashed across the sky.
This is to say the fog
of confusion crossed my mind.
And confusion, what do we know of its lives?
In the deadnight, in the scorch of moon
it rises on its spy legs,
howling a jinx.
That's what you hear when you think
wind.
And the wind, will it admit this?
It crawls it crawls
on the brown foothills,
mistraling a song.
Yesterday I heard the song twisting
the white birch and understood the sweet
cold lies, a child believing
everything she hears.

When I was young I thought a human
being was a legume
grown in the idea of birth.
I thought tarantula was the name
of death, living in the fruit of foreign countries.
I thought if you sat on the foothills
eating a banana
you could hear the dead walking on the other world.

Family Living in Abandoned Cave

Someone is writing a story with a stick
and someone is erasing it.

Dust is in the air,
and on their faces dust

gathers in a storm. *Rain
is falling*, a woman says, *it is falling*

still, and what is left on the wall
is thunder. Children are playing

in the corner by an unmade bed,
and on the table a pot of flowers.

A strange name is on the woman's lips:
Amittai, perhaps, and she wants to touch the man,

wants to press her tongue
to his skin, but the air is choking,

the children go on playing.
She is trying to remember the words of a story

she heard once about a man trapped
in a cave with his wife. In the darkness

he fashioned instruments with a bone and wood
and she sat playing music. She loved

the sound of his patient carving
and he loved her voice, but when they were found

it hurt him to see her body,
she hated his spider legs, his hair grown wild.

Then they were quiet. They never spoke.
In the slant of light children went on playing

games, drawing pictures in the dirt,
without malice.

1943

We never reached the camps.
Our lives sewn black onto our luggage,
we fled into the woods
where the stallion trees
frightened off the soldiers.
Above the birch the sun ran into sky
like a dab of paint on a watercolor,
but it never stormed, the clouds took pity.
When we reached the house of windows
I saw myself: a thin girl with a satchel—
and the sleeping room: glass dreams.
We unpacked our loaves of bread, told stories
and slept in each other's arms,
the trees behind us
vaguer than lost friends. I liked the woods
that spring, the needles and leaves under our feet
red and spongy, day after day
walking from the soldiers.

Sisters

For Malva

What was it like finding me
that day, wingdead, my face
blueing like a swallow?

Through the curtain did you see
the crimson
of the apple tree starting to move?

Or was it winter, the snowflakes
weakening against
a persuading white, my

voice gathering the last
air before your
scream?

How could I tell you to let
me go into the strange
bird, the absorbing

flight? You held on,
your small arms fastened
to the crib, more

than a mother.

Meanwhile it was summer.
The dunes breathed in and out
and a caravan of terns cruised across the sun—
the lighthouse with its foot in the water
tripped the black rocks— No
I'm not going to tell you
what we said, we were liars
and the thin hook of August
had us by the neck.

      My father forbid me to play
with Marina Velasquez. She had leukemia.
Her brothers and sisters brought her starfish
in jars and she set them on the front porch
and watched us run to the ocean.
And the ocean ran away from us,
so we swam in the little bays full of snails.
Hurricanes shook the boulders
loose in front of the house
and the bullets grayed
all the scorched faces called family,
except Grandma, napkin tucked into her blouse,
eating her plates of lobster
and staring into the fire.

      Then the boys
known as cousins gave us pistols and holsters
so we could fight like men, and we killed
each other over and over. I watched
them walk onto the beach
each dawn, whiteskins from the city
creeping up on the ocean
as if it were a bed
they could dive into, swimming
those clean velvet strokes
for which I have a weakness in my heart.

❦ Songs of an Ordinary Woman

I

When I was born Hannah was three
and Becky was born a year later.
We came over on the boat with the cheese,
like wood that cheese
but don't misunderstand me
you were lucky to get out.
There are no Litvaks now in Russia,
we had to leave and we came to Lowell.
We lived on Laskey's Block on River Street
with all the Jews
and what a home we had
oh boy oh boy!
My mother got us started,
she could cook she could bake
and very smart and clean and to this day
our people are the cleanest people.
My father was a ragpicker,
you have his picture with his little beard?
He was afraid a lot of times, everything
he was scared to death of.
Then there was a war you know
and Nattie Lerner, a singer,
he died in the war.
Etta and Bessie went for him
in a big way but he loved me
and said he did,
he tried so hard to be a singer
but the war
before our marriage,
he had such a nice voice,
there was a war you know.

II

A piano lesson in nineteen/nine,
now that was something,

that meant you were upper.
Lessons were 35¢ but who learned how to play?
By that time I liked the boys
and the boys liked me.
Imagine! Sixteen and a young man
rides from New York City,
a rich man and could dance
and handsome like all
New Yorkers and every day
I got a letter from Passaic.
My sister Hannah she couldn't find
no husband but they didn't sit around and sleep,
they made a match with Harry,
a nice boy but very homely.
A picnic at Kenoza Lake their wedding
and Harry wore a velvet cummerbund,
my father was ashamed.
When my turn came
we were already sweethearts.
The closest I ever got to Bernard
it was cold and winter,
he took my hand and put it in his pocket,
oh and he was squeezing it and warming it . . .
But his mother hated me,
she was jealous of the Litvaks.
Still he bought a trunk one day,
packed all his clothes and said to Hell
I'm getting married. His mother said
to Hell and burned the trunk
in the garden in Passaic.
Bernard rode the train to Lowell,
I hired my dress and we were off
to the Italian Club on River Street.
Such a happy wedding, the confetti and the band
and then the fun began, between the liquor
and the punching and the crying . . .

Grandmother

The man on the blue porcelain bowl
courts a woman,
white lace up her breasts,
her back arched lazily on a hoe.
Lynx eyes and candor.

My grandmother bought the bowl,
drank from it rich black tea.
She handed me a china story once:
the blue man
followed her; she took his gold rings,
babies and thick hands.

She learned to turn the earth.
From small stones bread grew,
the hard bulbs of vegetables
her offspring.

In winter her bones dried
and the husband drank old wine.

I have never seen
the house where he left her,
cerulean, the Russian soil.

In the Shoe Factory

It was easy to hypnotize the workers,
they always prefer roses to money.

So at Christmas before the strike
Esther trailed a chartreuse skirt

down the sawdust, a crepe blouse
unbuttoned to the stem of her bosom,

throwing petals on benches,
on rows of aproned boys, thin sticks of girls.

Then I brought in the beer and herring,
pumpernickel and sticky cakes.

Roses stood in thin-lipped vases
like ballerinas, while Esther played

the "Wassermusik" on a gramophone
and the "Tennessee Waltz" pulled workers into a ring

until men danced with men, fat girls in pumps
with girls, lights smoking overhead

like boiled Christmas eggs.
Outside snow grew in drifts of soot.

Dancing with Esther, the union manager
was drunk, she let him peek

at three crocheted buttons
sitting on her slip in buds

and I hummed into the flat ear of a girl,
pressing her close to my lapel.

At 6:00, too tired to vote for anything,
they filed sleepwalking into snow and we won.

The Boy Named Several

When I was five Jimmy Ornstein chased my sister
around the apple tree and caught her,
then we sat in a line and he combed her hair
while I combed his.

I barely remember my first boyfriend,
Buddy, stripping naked on the beach,
or Chucky waltzing me cheek to cheek
across the Sunday-school ballroom dance floor.

I was twelve when the boy at the back of the class fell
for me and all the hoods winked
voodoo from their desks and I was twenty
when he died of Hodgkin's.

I used to dream of saving
my boyfriends from murders
while the Ripper flew out a window
and my touch stitched a sliced throat.

Before my grandmother stopped talking
she always said: Marriage is
a girl's best friend, the loveliest days
of my life. Her husband

locked his family outside the house
one Christmas Eve and went on drinking;
it was snowing,
she was twenty-one.

When I open my drawer
the wooden letter box falls out

and I remember the sun on someone's
blond hair, and the boy named Denver

who cruised on coke
and the orphan from Germany
who threw himself in front of trucks
and now makes winter music.

When I look across the street
I see the young wife wiping her hands on an apron,
and the fence digs a story
into her yard: small girls pick violets

by the porch and give them
to a boyfriend, they are running
around a tree full of pink flowers,
one falls and the boy is kissing her. There's no way

to tell how the younger sister
feels, sitting on the grass,
her face is shaded
by huge leaves, I can't see her expression

as the boy combs her sister's hair
and she combs his.

✡ Marriage

He told me, You'll end up
a fat wife, wiping your hands
on an apron, your children outside a screen door
like geese flapping in the grain.
You'll have wrinkles
and veins on your legs, at night
little trumpets will sound in your ears,
bleating she-goats from a hillside
green with rain.

Your husband, he said,
will be strong as leather, always hungry,
the hairs on his face red
as clay. Mona,
he will call you, Mona my dear,
and you, pinching roses
into sallow cheeks, will wander
to his chair. Fights, oh yes,
wormholes in the plum tree,
lost animals, drought, death beneath a tractor . . .

   It's true
there are children in the bald fields,
I forget their ages. Today
one of the boys undressed
my youngest girl, her skin a white slip
of fur. In time they kiss
and marry, grow old and stout out here, turning
the black soil again and again in a memory
of love.

Norwegian Morning

The way a woman pours water
from pitcher to washbasin
on the morning
before slaughtering the hens
is empty as the bed she left,
though the man dreams of a fat
and kerchiefed woman, pushing a wheelbarrow
of potatoes to the barn.
As she watches her skin repel the water,
out in the yard
weather turns above the silo
and animals brew the dawn
with human sounds.
In the kitchen she lights
an electric bulb, her children
sleeping in their beds
like dark stones.
Just before winter
she slices sourdough bread,
smells the milk by the door
and begins to sew her linen.
It is almost morning,
outside
the white hens gather in a cloud of joy.

Over Here

The half-wits in the luncheonette walk past
in uniforms and smiles, the cups and saucers
in their racks their only sons and daughters—
I'm listening to their songs, their eyes unwashed
as infants' eyes—my eyes avert their stares.

Along the bench five women sit, their arms
locked into arms, as if marauders tossed
them there at Jordan's downtown crossing.
Their children rose on angel dust, and hearts
just stopped. Their husbands flew through Vietnam

spraying Agent Orange. Their losses rise
in Ireland now, the wee ones and the salts. . . .
They shift arthritic bones in Boston's laggard March
and dimestore flower merchants laugh and wink
at such old boats and such unkempt cargo.

I wear my life as if it were a gown
I hate to smirch or smear with dirty things.
The waitresses at Slagle's serve me tea
as if I were the Queen. I'm not refusing food
in Belfast or laying down my life for friends. . . .

What pain sears me, what nervous doubts
are smaller than the crumbs the pigeons nibble
on Milk Street, where they scratch the dirt
and fly in front of trucks and seem to clown,
such pale-faced beggars begging still, whose rage

       endures like privilege.

II

❊ The Air Between Two Deserts

Never the howling of humdrum moon
reminds me of you, nor the calamity of Tonto.
Not the black humor of Nijinsky's feet,
not music, my sometimes friend, nor the spell
of birds flying over to me.

Not the crenellated stars,
nor the sadness of ordinary devils.
Not the meditators in bathtubs,
the patrons of flophouses, the hotels
in Chinatown raping poppy merchants.

Not the first time in Exaltata's car,
nor the last cruise on Paradise Flats.
Not the amputee mailman home from the jungle
running on his hands,
not the lunatic runners high on Nirvana fumes.

Not the bisons bumping heads in the dark,
not the question walking out of bed
staring at computerized roses.
Not madness,
ridicule or shame.

But Beauty:
the kid leaning on a tractor in 1949,
not smiling, the angel poet.

Urracas

September rolling down over the hills
rattling her bones in a gunnysack
over the breath of the dying crabapples,
wet and exhausted on the ground.

Over the flowers of summer's last heat:
chamisa, malva, and asters climbing
the rocks and gullies, reaching their colors
into the same shades of sky. We pass

kindly through them. This winter we will not suffer.
I look and the sun still crows
and flaps its wings above the hills and then
the children ride their bicycles into it

down the loud hill by the red Studebaker
where the lovers are leaning and waiting
for dark. We turn full circle and everywhere
it's land lusting for itself and we walk

the dirt road home and suddenly
under trees we hear them:
Rivers of birds No! Rapids
or falls, a roar

of thousands singing. Some, afraid, fly
into the air. They're falling in love! I know
these birds, they'll knave a cat into the woods,
peck out windows. Small boys

learning to hate catch them in nets
and slice their tongues in half
and teach them to speak
our language, our poor human language.

Rapture

When they finished there was nothing
but a mute girl at the front
trying to speak. They shook their hands
over her head like dried leaves
but it wouldn't do any good.
The organist swelled her psalms
and the congregation shook with fever
in their midnight drawl that went on
and on until the pews grew fungus
and people walked home in the electric air
that hit the mountains and bounced back.

        So the girl
knew her time was up and started
braying at the altar, shaking
in her yellow cotton dress
and knifing the poor drizzle outside
with rapture. Then the rain really came down
and the lightning took itself seriously.
I know what she said. I've heard it
a million times before
and it's not good news.

❧ It Seemed a Shame

In just a little while across these mountains
I'm going to stop the car
and walk through the fields of lupine and paintbrush.
They look so lovely sitting in their white fog
as if someone decided to wax them
and little droplets issued
from the clouds.

That's what they say about Auschwitz now.
It seemed a shame not to preserve
the surroundings, so they called it The Museum.
On fine days you can see the picnickers
on bright wool blankets
lift their cameras and stand on tiptoe
for the best shots, and the children
run on the grass and pick wildflowers that sit
in bottles in the hotel. Sometimes they forget
to water them or the maids carelessly
tip the jars or spray them,
and the children must beg their fathers
for better souvenirs from the shop,
things that will last longer.

❧ Garden

The girls in the garden
are crossing and uncrossing their legs
Like swans their thin white cotton dresses
lift and flap in the breeze

Small silvery insects crawl up and down
the arms of the girls in the garden
or walk across their foreheads
or ride past on the lace wings of dragonflies

It's so hot in the afternoon sun
you would think that the skin
of the girls in the garden
would shine with perpetual beads

and you can see them brush away
the silky bangs from their eyes
as they lift tall icy glasses
not moving
toward the scones and marmalade on the white settee

No one hears the words of the girls
as they lean like an indolent
predawn aviary
and invisible boys
running on the grass before them
trace concentric circles of green

Now they stand and stretch
and their T-strapped sandals
seem bird footprints on a beach
as the sky turns aluminum

and the girls walk together
through the cream and magenta
roses outlining the house

It's too late
to warn them of the dark
scar starting in the hills
when they're barefoot on the new wet lawn
and I'm yelling please go in the thunder
the rain
They can't hear me and I see
only soaked skirts clinging

as the storm sends down its pins
and the yard and the night are one
black motion as the girls
in the garden swing translucent
dresses around their immutable bones
Why are they doing it
Are they indestructible
Girls like saplings
no foothold in this world

Mr. Yee Is in the Garden

Mr. Yee is in the garden talking to his flowers.
I don't know what he says
but I know they love him, little boats
coming to anchor in his hands.

He weeds and laughs. The thin notes
of a song glide across the soil, dark
as the Chinese fishing village
he hasn't seen in thirty years.

And beyond the muddy river, in the next town,
Dusk slides into its car and speeds
through the red light by the depot
and arrives in its pale coat.

Sails gather in the gray:
orange tiger lilies,
roses and the fragile
pink bleeding hearts.

Mr. Yee is singing them to sleep.
On the roof the sun balances on its back.
He stands watchful, hands on his hips.
Anything could snatch them.

Small Concrete Objects
and a Sailing Thing

It's Saturday night and Mr. Yee lost his key,
so we're watching television in my front room.
Two blond children on the sidewalk push each other
in a wheelbarrow and a rain
has just started to fall
on all the things growing in the gutters
when a famous actor claiming to be one-sixteenth
Indian comes on the screen.
He talks about exploitation and then
the screen fills with all the cowboys and horses
I watched from my armchair as a child
and a silent film called "The Savage Child" shows an Indian girl
teasing a young soldier in the woods as she curls around
a tree and bats her lashes
until the boy can't stand it any longer
and grabs her and then we're at a reservation in New Mexico
and Mr. Yee is saying,
Why don't the Jews believe in a soul?

.   .   .   .

I'm afraid to tell him to be quiet
and watch the program, so I listen to him
link the Jews and the Jehovah's Witnesses
in refusing to believe in life after death
and he says, *What's this life anyway*
compared to a soul that goes on and on.
I think of the newsprint pamphlets
left on my doorstep and once a hand-scrawled note
said I would be saved
at four o'clock on Sunday
and then she told me that she loved me.
The walls started falling in that year
in Philadelphia, so I returned to Boston,

to Feldman's bakery with its electric sign
and poppy-seed cakes from when I was a child
staring at the skinny red-haired woman,
at the pale blue number on her arm.
I'm an old man, Mr. Yee is saying, *an old old man.*
My wife pours vinegar on me—
She wants to kill the young maple
outside your window she thinks will ruin the foundation,
she might as well pull me up by the roots. . . .
And then he's on his feet,
he's off to feed his chickens on the porch,
and walks bowing and hunched into the scoundrel night,
wounded savior of all growing things.

Mr. Yee Feeds the Pigeons

1.

The cars in the municipal parking lot
look bald as old women trying to pray
in an empty church.
Over the bedroom curtains I see them
leaning into sunlight, afraid to move
their brittle bones for fear they'd crack.

Someone is whistling upstairs
a low desolate tune of Manchuria
and outside the trees wail in the wind
and walk on new red claws,
while for us just rising from each other
is a perilous journey.

2.

Mr. Yee rakes the old leaves
from the azaleas—
He bustles below my window
bent over in a cap,
all morning laughing and joking
with the black-and-blue pigeons he knows so well.

All April down on his knees
throwing the birds orange peels and bread crumbs.
He's smiling, it's
Easter Sunday.
In just a little while he'll lift his cap and ask me
am I afraid to die?

3.

I drum my fingers down your back
and dream of the house we'll build
and then the lights go out,
Beethoven fades. Mr. Yee and you
walk down to the cellar armed with candles
like a father and son.

He says he's lost his daughter. In spiked high-
heels she disco dances, stays out all night—
The Puerto Rican's dragon car pulls up
and he won't speak to her. She's dead.
You touch the lily's stem.
I trust a man who likes flowers, he says.

✠ Like Wings

For Thomas

The gaudy magpie clouds
steal over the Sangre de Christos
and land above my head
and wilt and fly over the sleeping dogs
till I yell, Chula, Zia! Look up!
But they're galloping in their dreams
through healthy rain splashing the grass
and filling the gullies with brown juice.
Soon the rain will start inside me,
soon I'll drill through the arroyo heart
and the river of old snow will crash
and the low riders stare crawling by
and the Harleys rock back and forth
watching tears fall on the wooden porch chair
and land on the comfrey and mint
and water the sage and the long dirty road I live on.
Camelback clouds will open
and spiders climbing thin air will hide
and the nettle and the Oriental poppies
will lean toward the water. Hey!
I'm washing the valley! Tears cruise
Montoya to Paseo del Pueblo
past Our Lady of Guadalupe, crying in her plaza,
who knows I'm like the old woman
hanging out sheets on the line and wanting
to hang myself out too—
Tired of mirrors lining the walls
and mistrust refusing to sweep itself out
with the morning dust, and fear creeping
around my feet like cats
and all the old proverbs standing in the corner,

as always, laughing—
stranding me on the lowland
instead of ascending the delicate wind-swept hills of Talpa
where I could lift up my elbows and fly . . .

       Down below I see the men
touching themselves through thin trousers
and sipping paper bags at noon,
on Sunday walking from the Assembly of God
Pentecostal Church on my corner . . .
      I see the tears
riding the grooves of Romolo's face
as he speaks of the New Year's Eve plane crash
and friends vanished over these mountains
like his brother trampled by the bison
when he was a boy.
He saw the herd ten thousand times,
he saw white bones the wind blew through.
He says the trees give song when someone dies
and you have to learn to hear the leaves
and he sits down with his face in his hands
while outside the stars tread water
like tiny faithful swimmers.

III

Freeze Tag

"Rabbi, rabbi, where is God?" the little boy asked.

"Everywhere," answered the rabbi. "There is no place empty of Him, so whatever you do, you couldn't fool Him."

"Is God in our cellar?" the boy asked.

"Oh yes, bubeleh, He is certainly in your cellar."

"Ha, ha," the little boy said. "I fooled you. We got no cellar."

—*Barbara Myerhoff*

NUMBER OUR DAYS

1   Hayyim Tells the Trees

Sometimes in winter
I get this urge.
I walk in the woods
and all the trees look dead, no insects
crawl up and down their backs, their arms
out stiff. I think I know them—
this sounds crazy—
I say, Hello, Schlomo!
Remember me?
Hi, Sammie, Abie . . .
I lie down there
under one of those old buddies
and I sleep in the snow.
There's no one to bother me; my wife
at the house piles her laundry
with an angry face,
my daughter gone to the city.
I slip underground,
I'm with my brothers,
I like it.
And all the shoe factories in the damn Northeast
can rot for all I care—
I'm sick and tired of leather and nails.

God help me
if I think of nothing but my poor mother,
for whose sake my hands turned brown from dye.
She'd take them in her warm ones and knead them,
she'd sell her braids for me
if I was hungry. A wife
can turn
but a mother's a mother her whole life.

Now I'm an old man who will die
but you're born and you die,
that's it.
I should be happy for waking up

with my two arms and my two legs.
My mouth speaks, it praises God.
My eyes work, they stare at the sun
and water begins to fall. . . .

Another sniffling face going around
asking God for everything—
a little food on the table, a little fun—
and what does God say?

I'd go to the trees, these black branches,
before I'd go to Him.
When I call Him, God faces me
with a closed door.

2   Freeze Tag

When I was a boy outside Kiev
we'd play a little game, freeze tag.
Wings on your feet, you ran
until the guy covering his eyes said,
                Freeze!
You couldn't budge, you stopped breathing.
I never moved a muscle,
they never caught me.
There was a little kid, my friend Yakov.
Once, playing in the middle of town at dusk,
the soldiers came, it was 1908.
We scrammed out of there fast,
flew from the big boots and bayonets
to any house we knew.
Only Yakov, frozen like a statue
behind the firehouse, held his breath,
his eyes shut, in another world.
We had a special name, we called them
the stolen.
I was nine and I was strong
but they grabbed and made a soldier of a six-year-old.

3   Shalom, Nosovka

Things got bad, then things got worse.
It gives me the horrors to think of this.
The Cossacks ripped our houses to shreds
and whitened the streets with our feather beds
till you thought it was winter.
We played in the drifts
and the old people cried
into the strange snow, combing for treasures and teeth.
Mother wrote letters to relatives
and sent me to town to sell the cow. She knew
what I was up to, stepsister
with the solemn eyes.
I looked at her
and she looked at me—
you couldn't tell who was worse off.
In my basket with a lid and napkin I hid
grandfather's gold watch, found in the feathers,
mine when I turned thirteen.
They eat cows
across the ocean, grandfather told me.
They drink blood
and they worship money.
I stopped dead in my tracks
at the market boiling with hawkers and thieves,
my arms around the cow,
a skinny kid they couldn't fill up.
She was my first mistress
and old chum, mother of butter
and milk for pudding, lugger of burdens
sitting tethered now to the cart
of Isaac the goldsmith.
I walked home alone, eyes glued
to the clouds fleeing a hungry sun.
I walked alone with kopecks in my basket.
They eat cows in America, he said. . . .
If I didn't save her neck,

I vowed, God should run me over
not once but a hundred times
with poor Krepsky's milk wagon.

✡ 4   Many Waters Cannot Drown It

They couldn't fill me up.
I slept above the stove.
My younger sister, Rachele, the dybbuk,
saved crusts of bread in a napkin
and like I was a bird
popped them at night into my mouth.
Amazing how many hours we sat up
talking about crossing that ocean
and how Heschel, the oldest,
handy with a needle and thread,
would land there first.
Those nights if I leaned over
I could touch her red curls
hanging on a muslin nightgown.
I could touch the bare feet
she sat fingering.
Somehow she knew
without that black bread
I thought I'd starve.
If I close my eyes
I can see her still climbing down
that huge stove to her trundle.
And never again,
not in seventy-six years,
have I seen a love that thick,
with a butcher knife
you couldn't even cut it.

5   Isle of Hope, Isle of Tears

You can go into the gypsy camp,
but the bears do the Kazotskhi on your stomach.

We land and they said it was an island.
So tired my eyelids wouldn't obey.
And on a square piece of floor
my first night in America
I dreamed I lost
the paper they pinned to my coat,
I lost the scarf around my neck, my trousers,
my black scuffed shoes and prayer book,
I lost my parents and brother and sister
and down a long dark corridor I ran
from fat officers
pulling their mustaches.

There was a wind
and the wind spoke
sucking me to its middle   *What is your name*
        Did you pay your way   Are you an anarchist

    I saw officers
snatching my sister, I ran
to stop them, they twisted my arms
behind my back . . . my sister turned into
    a hen, hatchet in their hands
        they placed her on a rock
                If you want her
                do a dance

        Little boy, do a mazurka

I forgot the steps but I twirled around
    I wanted to please them   *Little boy*
        they smirked   *Sing a song for us*

I opened my mouth   I remembered the anthem
    I opened my mouth but no sound came out. . . .

43

What is your name   Did you pay your passage
I shrank smaller
     and smaller and then I was in Europe
          swimming to my family
               on the other side, eating dirty sausages at a long wooden
               table in a cellar   I swam

with legs like blocks of ice   I swam
and I got nowhere   I saw needles
poking my father's eyes   I saw officers plucking
a bright red hen   I swam
and shrank into a nothing
a cipher
a thimble my brother could've hidden
in the pocket of his coat.

6   The Boy Falling Out of the Boy's Head
          Any rags, any bones
          any bottles today?
          The same old story
          in the same old way.

My father, may he rest in peace,
was a timid man, a tiny man,
he never bothered no one.
A ragman, singing into the morning
with his team and wagon,
graybeard into gray . . .

My father, may he rest in peace.
          One Saturday
Father, Rachele and me
strolled down the street
minding our own business
when a big fella in back
kicks my father and starts to laugh:

"Dirty kike, dirty kike!
Go back where you came from!"

Father didn't know the punching game—
in Russia he got punched around himself—
so my heart skipped to see him crash
into the belly of that big swine. . . . Next
thing I knew we met the street, blood
on our faces, seeing stars, and I'd give anything for a shot
of schnapps . . . my legs crying, Father flat
and my sister screaming from the back of her throat

    "I'll give you a penny stop it I'll give you
        a penny . . ."

               In that split second
I see our people . . . Turtles
in every land, carting our nation
on our backs

      Soft in the morning
go the wheels of Father's wagon.
   In every country we learn to listen.

7   **Hayyim's Luck**

Like Max rushing the morning's bagels
to Foxie's Deli 5 a.m.
my father on a hot day in June
rushed to his last breath.
When he stopped with the cigarettes
the pneumonia took over.
By then we weren't rich
but we weren't poor neither.
When the schoolbell rang every afternoon
I shot out to the street

selling newspapers, it was quite a thing
a kid twelve years old who couldn't
even talk English to go out and sell papers
no matter what the weather.
I made maybe six, seven bucks a week,
gave my mother five and kept the rest
to go with boyfriends and have some fun.
But a coupla kids liked to give me trouble.
One Polack liked to steal my papers.
Once I let him catch up
and turned around and knocked him down
and told him, "If you don't beat it, I'll break your back!"
From that time on he knew what was coming.
We got along quite nice with my papers
and my brother sewing in a shop
and every Shabbas, kreplach swimming in the chicken soup.
Then in '17 the war
and I was water boy at the army camp
making more money than I ever saw.
We knew what devils drowned the old country, we tried
not to think . . .
Like a seven-year rain
all our relations and friends over there
just washed away.

אַ־שׁ 8   **Shayner Maidele**

I wearied of the singsong music of the shul,
the drone of Hebrew for the daily prayers.
Hmph! I said, I'd rather get a job.

Sixteen years old I walked with the black coats
to the shoe factory on the river.
In that place machines have voices
and the minute I entered I knew the language.

Our slipper city made hand-turned shoes
like French kid gloves

mulled in steam and hammered to a last—
the most beautiful shoes in America!

I didn't mind the noise and dust,
the wagging finger of the foreman, and every job
in the shop—cutting and lasting,
stitching and finishing—in two years every job I mastered.

With everyone I got along
but the Jews and Poles and Greeks and Irish
like screeching monkeys
forced to live on the same tree
kept to their own branches.

I sat next to, in the stitching room,
Mrs. Piroushka and she liked me,
brought me candies and cakes from the Polish holidays.

And then one day she brought a picture—
and set it under my nose—
of her sister's oldest daughter. . . .
       The hair pulled off her face,
the high cheekbones of a lady, when she came to the factory
her piled-up auburn hair
       took my breath. . . .

              I was eighteen, I had
no business falling for a girl,
I didn't know love could crawl under your skin
and take over, or kill
the work your fingers used to do, I didn't know
you could hear her voice and no other,
and for this I called her
       Shayner Maidele,
because she was my beautiful young girl.

   We met in secret that winter. I gave her
little gifts, a piece of fruit, some candy,

and then my mother caught on.
    "A Polish girl?
            Hayyim, devils dance on your father's grave
for this!"

I knew she was right
and I knew she was wrong,
the sticks and stones
fighting in my stomach tore me up,
I wanted to ask someone
but who could you ask?
I listened for the right thing to do,
I pressed my ear to the ground
                    Deaf music!

        But then it didn't matter—
The lips I never dared to kiss,
the voice like an angel's,
    the slow dance of her skirt
                    moving across the floor
stopped.
            My Rosa caught the fever.

To fall from a great height
is a terrible thing.
Falling from clouds is worse—
I lived but I didn't live, I
turned to stone.

For this I left women alone
for twelve years.
I worked myself to the bone, I gave
to my family, I saved up.

But love, that fragile spirit
in a man's life,
she calls once, she don't
call twice.

I broke down   I left work
I couldn't eat   I couldn't sleep
and no one could comfort me.

✿ 9   Hayyim Flies Over

In the hive and in the anthill
the female rules
and the same in my house.
Everywhere you looked, scissors and ruffles
and lace and bows and Mother
scrubbing the kitchen floor every day,
my sister worrying after me,
challah growing every Friday in the brass bowl
and leaving the oven, a miracle,
the kitchen smelling of tsimmes and chicken livers,
the table set with a white cloth . . .

                              You can't say a blessing

over an unlit candle.
I came back to life.
When we walked into town
people bowed;
they said I was chosen, they said
I was destined, God willing,
to do wonderful things.

✿ 10   An Only Daughter

Nothing stood as upright as I, hands jammed
into mittens, ears into a cap, that morning
I walked back into the sawdust smell—
Old pals left their benches to clap
me on the back—"Long time no see!"

I feared I would forget how to draw
on leather. No fool was I—
Before I knew it I owned
a shoeshop on River Street,
workers piling in by the droves.

I used them well, no complaints made the smokestacks
shiver and die out,
I was the boss of a hearty company.
And still the long nights I couldn't sleep
in my sister's house, grandfathering her young family.

And then one night I met a girl name of Sonya
at a Blossoms of Zion social.
I took her to a moving picture
and in the dark held her hand
and knew she was both shy and clever.

In no time at all I persuaded her
to marry me,
we honeymoon'd in Miami Beach,
I did everything I could
to erase the other from my memory.

And then the gift from heaven,
the luckiest day of my life,
day the poor man and the rich
recognize each other, we had a child—
    The old pain flew out the window, in came

    a beautiful fair-haired daughter.

11 The Hermit's Hut

> I am a brother to dragons and a companion
> to owls. . . .
> My harp also is turned to mourning and my organ
> into the voice of them that weep.
>
> —JOB

I am the garment that is moth-eaten and the prisoner
in the stocks.
The wind whips and the dirt chases me.

Tu tu, I spit over my shoulder
to cast off the evil eye.

I lie at night in my narrow bed
beside the empty bed of my wife
and she's downstairs watching television,
mooning over Gable or Bogart
and I'm reading a magazine
and getting in a mood. . . .

I haven't had my wife, you understand,
it seems like years.
I'm lying alone in the room
and the walls wind around me
like a skein of yarn.
I can't breathe,
I'm smothered,
and she's watching a late movie.

I walk around in the dark and stumble
like a drunken man and ask her, When
are you coming to bed, and she says, Soon. . . .
I could wait for the sands to polish me.

The Angel of Death with folded wings
sits beside me, laughing,

and I cry, I'm a man!
I'm a man! And a man has a heart
that can snap in two.

And the white-shrouded night lies down with me
and holds my hand in her lap,
I am her child, no, her dog. . . .

How do you stop the skin from hunger?
How do you say, just go to sleep!

I fear for my life and for my body
like I'm walking through the desert
with unquenchable thirst—
I don't know why the Lord cursed me like this:
My own wife is my enemy.

12   And It Came to Pass

The Bible says you should live to see
your children's children,
you should come to the grave in a full age,
as a shock of corn
ripens in its season,
and I knew it was time to wish
not for myself but for my daughter,
the flower growing so quick
and lovely in bad soil.

I sat in my den day after day
watching the weather go by,
turning the pages of magazines
and flipping the TV dial.

I sat day after day
plotting her dowry
and counting my rows of shoes.

What I could do for her made me dizzy
with joy, in my life where nothing mattered—
this wealth a tree of comfort to me.

✳ 13   Forgetting

It started small. I'd go
to the store for something
then lose track,
I'd have to call.
And then it got to be I was scared
to drive the car
for fear I'd lose the way, you don't know
where it hides, memory,
that long blue drink—
What good are years
if the mind walks away?

The day I forgot
the pot of milk
she lashed her shoulder at me. I bet
she wished it was a knife. Lemme
do it, I said, I'll clean up the stove.
What's the matter? she said. Huh?
What's the matter with you, can't you
remember anything?

✳ 14   Gone

I have a picture.

There's a cabin in the woods
A woman stands in the window
ladling a cup of tea   she's wearing
a blue housedress   hair tied

in a babushka   she's slicing
a loaf of black bread   trees with leaves
the color of rubies sway in the breeze—

No breeze. It's gone.
And the woman who couldn't even speak
the new language.
And my brother and sister.
Dozens of names falling into the grate
like spring rain. People who made out
like bandits and men of clean spirit,

my buddies, Harry and Abie,
Schlomo and Sam.
It hurts your eyes
like staring into the noonday sun. . . .

   And you know you will go soon
and prepare yourself and tread
lightly on the soil. . . .

      It's ready and has a hunger for you.

15   No History Like Feet

    Pain comes in with knotty hands,
it walks with broken feet.
Pain is the country I live in.

    When I take off my shoes, the toes
are crying, when I pull off my socks
the soles yell, and the heels
are laughingstocks, crumbling
into parchment.

Where am I going with this cane,
a brand-new foot?

I make a fist, it's a wing.

I jump up, a bird.

Runaway in the sky, far above the city and
someone yells out, Hayyim! Hayyim!
    They can't sue you
    for trying!

About the Author

Marea Gordett grew up in Haverhill, in a family of Russian immigrants. She began writing poetry in the fifth grade and continued through high school and college at the University of Pennsylvania (B. A., 1971) and at the University of Massachusetts/Amherst (M. F. A., 1979). She won the Discovery/*The Nation* award (1979), the Pushcart Prize V (1980–1981), and received a grant from the Helene Wurlitzer Foundation (1984). She lives in Boston.

About the Book

Freeze Tag has been composed in Bodoni Book by G & S Typesetters of Austin, Texas; it was printed on 60 pound Gladfelter by McNaughton & Gunn Lithographers of Ann Arbor, Michigan.